P9-EIE-796

WITHDRAWN

ANIMALS AND THEIR HABITATS
Savannas

WORLD
BOOK

A Scott Fetzer company
Chicago
www.worldbookonline.com

World Book, Inc.
233 N. Michigan Avenue
Chicago, IL 60601
U.S.A.

For information about other World Book publications, visit our website at http://www.worldbookonline.com or call 1-800-WORLDBK (967-5325).

For information about sales to schools and libraries, call 1-800-975-3250 (United States), or 1-800-837-5365 (Canada).

Staff

Executive Committee
President: Donald D. Keller
Vice President and Editor in Chief: Paul A. Kobasa
Vice President, Marketing/Digital Products: Sean Klunder
Vice President, International: Richard Flower
Controller: Yan Chen
Director, Human Resources: Bev Ecker

Editorial

Associate Director, Supplementary Publications:
  Scott Thomas
Managing Editor, Supplementary Publications:
  Barbara A. Mayes
Associate Manager, Supplementary Publications:
  Cassie Mayer
Editors: Brian Johnson and Kristina Vaicikonis
Researcher: Annie Brodsky
Editorial Assistant: Ethel Matthews
Manager, Contracts & Compliance
  (Rights & Permissions): Loranne K. Shields
Indexer: David Pofelski
Writer: David Alderton
Project Editor: Sarah Uttridge
Editorial Assistant: Kieron Connolly
Design: Andrew Easton

Graphics and Design

Senior Manager: Tom Evans
Senior Designer: Don Di Sante
Manager, Cartography: Wayne K. Pichler
Senior Cartographer: John Rejba

Pre-Press and Manufacturing

Director: Carma Fazio
Manufacturing Manager: Steven K. Hueppchen
Senior Production Manager: Janice Rossing
Production/Technology Manager: Anne Fritzinger
Proofreader: Emilie Schrage

Library of Congress Cataloging-in-Publication Data
Savannas.
    p. cm. -- (Animals and their habitats)
  Includes index.
  Summary: "Illustrations and text in this nonfiction volume introduce some of the animals commonly found in savannas. Detailed captions describe each animal, while inset maps show where they live. Special features include a glossary, photographs, and an index"--Provided by publisher.
  ISBN 978-0-7166-0443-3
  1. Savanna animals--Juvenile literature. I. World Book, Inc.
QL115.3.S285 2012
591.7'48--dc23
                    2012005841

Animals and Their Habitats
Set ISBN 978-0-7166-0441-9

Printed in China by Leo Paper Products, LTD.,
Heshan, Guangdong
1st printing July 2012

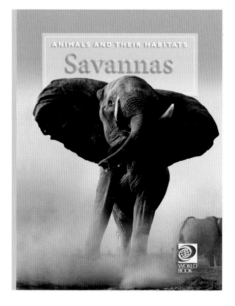

Cover image: An elephant charges across a savanna in Africa, which has more grassland animals than any other area. Savannas throughout the world are home to great herds of grazers, ferocious meat-eaters, and amazing birds, both large and small.

© Alamy (Steve Bloom Images)

Contents

Introduction

The savanna (also spelled *savannah*) is home to an amazing variety of wildlife. Some of Earth's most magnificent animals live on the savanna, including elephants, giraffes, lions, and zebras. The savanna is a grassland with widely scattered shrubs and trees. The climate is usually warm, and there is typically a wet and a dry season.

The most celebrated savanna is found on the plains of Africa. Savanna covers more than two-fifths of the continent. Savannas also cover parts of Australia, India, North America, and South America. These areas all provide similar *habitat* (the type of place in which an animal lives).

BATELEUR EAGLE

The savanna is a place of extremes. During the dry season, food and water can be hard to find. Rivers may dry to a trickle. Animals may be forced to gather around shrinking waterholes, providing an endless feast for hungry *predators* (hunting animals). Grass turns brown and dies. Great brush fires race through the dry vegetation. During the wet season, sudden downpours can cause flash floods, which carry animals away in swollen rivers. But the rains support abundant grass, and animals thrive.

The savanna is home to great herds of *grazing* (grass-eating) animals, including an incredible diversity of antelopes. These animals often leap gracefully as they flee predators, almost seeming to taunt them. The savanna also supports great herds of wildebeests and zebras. These herds *migrate* (travel from place to place) with the rains, searching for the lush grass they need to support their numbers. The herds are followed by fearsome predators. The jaws of hyenas can crack open bones. Lions hunt in groups called prides, working together to take down prey.

LION

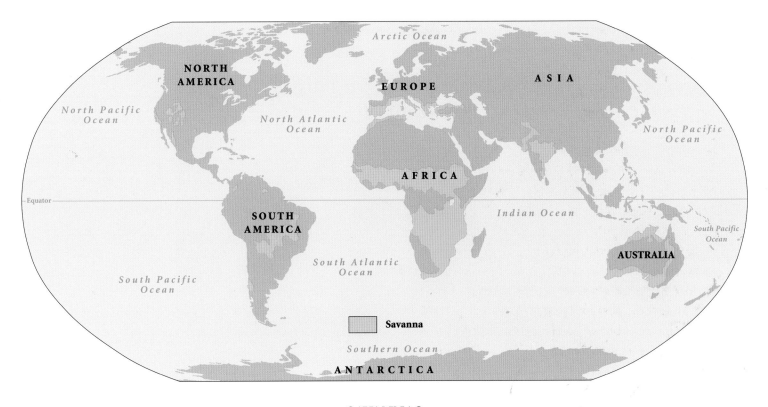

SAVANNAS

MEERKAT

Some animals of the savanna depend on trees. Elephants can use their trunks to pull down branches. Giraffes, with their long necks, are able to reach up and feed in the treetops.

Many animals of the savanna take advantage of the openness of the land. The bateleur (pronounced *bat LERR*) eagle soars high above the grass, relying on its keen eyesight to spot prey. A snake caught in its sharp talons has little chance of escape. As the largest living bird, the ostrich cannot fly. Instead, its strong legs propel it to great speeds in the open country, enabling it to outrun most predators. But no animal runs faster than the cheetah. The fastest land animal on Earth, the cheetah can reach speeds of 50 to 70 miles (80 to 110 kilometers) per hour over short distances. Even a swift gazelle cannot rely on speed alone to escape.

Impala

SPECIES • *Aepyceros melampus*

The impala is an African antelope known for its swift, graceful jumping and running. An impala may travel 30 feet (9 meters) in a single leap. It can run at up to 50 miles (80 kilometers) per hour.

VITAL STATISTICS

WEIGHT	About 100–176 lb (45–80 kg)
HEIGHT	33–37 in (84–94 cm) at shoulder; males larger than females
SEXUAL MATURITY	2 years
LENGTH OF PREGNANCY	7–8 months; longer if conditions are harsh
NUMBER OF OFFSPRING	1; can be born at any time of year in equatorial Africa
DIET	Eats fresh grass when available, as well as leaves and shoots at other times
LIFESPAN	12–15 years maximum

WHERE IN THE WORLD?

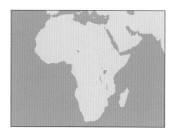

Lives in eastern and southern Africa.

ANIMAL FACTS

Impalas instinctively feed both by *grazing* (eating grasses) at ground level and also by browsing on taller plants, particularly when grass is hard to find during dry spells of weather. They tend not to stray far from water. Males establish territories with herds of females, and mating takes place at the end of the wet season. The female later breaks away from the herd, giving birth alone. Mother and fawn then rejoin the group. Fawns stop nursing about six months later.

A clash of horns between males

DANGEROUS ACQUAINTANCES

Cheetahs can outrun impalas. Lions, wild dogs, and hyenas also represent a serious threat, especially if hunting in groups.

HORNS
Only the male impala, known as a ram, has long, ridged, S-shaped horns. These can grow to 36 inches (91 centimeters) in length.

SENSES
Impalas have a keen sense of smell and hearing and sharp eyesight.

COLORATION
Reddish-brown with paler underside and black markings.

LEGS
An impala's slender but powerful legs give it speed and grace.

HOW BIG IS IT?

Springbok

VITAL STATISTICS

WEIGHT	70–100 lb (32–45 kg)
LENGTH	56–65 in (142–165 cm)
SEXUAL MATURITY	1–2 years
LENGTH OF PREGNANCY	About 171 days, with births most common between October and December at the start of the wet season
NUMBER OF OFFSPRING	1
DIET	Eats both grass and shrubs, according to the season
LIFESPAN	Maximum 7–10 years in the wild

ANIMAL FACTS

A springbok may leap into the air repeatedly, a behavior known as *stotting* or *pronking*. Scientists are not sure why the springbok does this, especially as it slows the animal down when *predators* (hunting animals) are chasing it. Some scientists think pronking advertises the springbok's health and strength, discouraging predators from further pursuit. When many members of the herd leap at once, it may confuse predators.

Long eyelashes protect the eyes in tall grass.

The name *springbok* refers to this animal's great leaping ability. The springbok can "spring" up to 6 ½ feet (2 meters) into the air. It also runs gracefully, at up to 55 miles (89 kilometers) per hour.

WHERE IN THE WORLD?

Lives in remote parts of southwestern Africa, including open country in Angola, Botswana, and Namibia, as well as on reserves and farms in South Africa.

HORNS
Both sexes have horns, but they are stouter and longer in adult males, growing up to 19 inches (48 centimeters) in length.

EARS
The long, narrow ears turn easily in all directions, helping to detect potential danger.

HINDQUARTERS
This part of the springbok's body is higher than the shoulders.

LEGS
The forelegs are straight and slender.

HOW BIG IS IT?

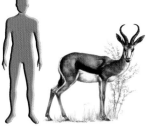

REACHING UP
By supporting its weight on its hindquarters, the springbok is able to graze on higher branches.

Thomson's Gazelle

VITAL STATISTICS

WEIGHT	29–66 lb (13–30 kg); males are heavier
LENGTH	42–56 in (106–142 cm), including tail; up to 35 in (90 cm) tall
SEXUAL MATURITY	Females 8–14 months; males 11–12 months
LENGTH OF PREGNANCY	155–186 days; weaned 4 months later
NUMBER OF OFFSPRING	1
DIET	Feeds on grass and other vegetation
LIFESPAN	10–15 years in the wild; up to 20 in captivity

ANIMAL FACTS

Like other gazelles, these animals are fast, reaching speeds up to 50 miles (80 kilometers) per hour. Even so, they can be outrun by cheetahs over short distances. Fawns are especially vulnerable to *predators* (hunting animals), and roughly half of them die before reaching maturity. This danger-filled existence may explain why females give birth twice rather than once a year. The numbers of these gazelles have declined in recent years.

Thomson's gazelle is also known for the kind of leaping known as stotting or pronking.

These gazelles often travel alongside great herds of wildebeests and zebras. All of these animals follow the rains during the wet season, to take advantage of the abundant grass that grows.

WHERE IN THE WORLD?

Lives in East Africa, in Ethiopia, Sudan, and particularly in southern and central Kenya and northern Tanzania.

HORNS
The horns spiral along their length, with the tips pointing forward. They are much longer in males, measuring up to 12 inches (30 centimeters) long.

EARS
Ears are long and set well back on the head; they have black insides.

COLORATION
Light brown, with distinctive black stripes on the sides and a white underside.

FACIAL FEATURES
The eyes are encircled with white markings, forming a stripe down the nose.

HOW BIG IS IT?

COURTSHIP

Male Thomson's gazelles establish territories at 2 years old. Females move through such territories and linger in the ones with good grazing.

Topi

VITAL STATISTICS

WEIGHT	287–375 lb (130–170 kg); females are lighter
LENGTH	5–6.8 ft (1.5–2 m), including tail
SEXUAL MATURITY	Females from 1.5 years; males from 3 years, but will not breed for at least another year
LENGTH OF PREGNANCY	About 248 days
NUMBER OF OFFSPRING	A single offspring, typically weaned by 1 year old
DIET	Grazes exclusively on grass
LIFESPAN	12–15 years average

ANIMAL FACTS

The topi prefers flood plains to drier ground, as it is more likely to find fresh, lush grass growing there. It is social by nature, living in groups of about 20, though herds of up to 100 individuals have been observed during *migration* (moving from place to place). Like many other grazers of the savanna, the topi follows the rains to find plentiful grass. Males fight to control groups of females. When running, topis have a bounding gait. The topi is also known as the *tsessebe*.

Female topi and young

Topi calves alter their behavior depending on conditions. When lush grass supports large herds, calves seek safety in numbers. When herds are smaller, the mother and her calf leave to hide among the trees.

WHERE IN THE WORLD?

Ranges from Senegal to Ethiopia and down to South Africa; especially numerous in southern Sudan and Tanzania, in the Serengeti National Park.

EARS
The long, flexible ears offer warnings of such potential *predators* (hunting animals) as lions and leopards.

MOUTHPARTS
The jaws are narrow, reflecting the fact that these animals feed only on grass.

HORNS
Horns are ringed and bent, growing to about 21 inches (53 centimeters) long.

COLORATION
Topis are instantly recognizable by the distinctive dark markings on their bodies. Females tend to be lighter in color.

A MUD BATH
Topis will roll in damp mud, smearing it all over their bodies, probably as a means of keeping cool.

HOW BIG IS IT?

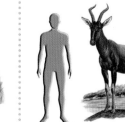

Kirk's Dik-Dik

VITAL STATISTICS

WEIGHT	6–14.5 lb (2.7–6.5 kg)
LENGTH	23–32.5 in (59–83 cm), including the tail
SEXUAL MATURITY	Females from 6–8 months and males between 8–9 months
LENGTH OF PREGNANCY	From 155–186 days, with births occurring in two main periods each year
NUMBER OF OFFSPRING	1
DIET	Eats grasses, leaves, and flowers
LIFESPAN	About 10 years

ANIMAL FACTS

These small antelopes face many *predators* (hunting animals), including baboons, cheetahs, eagles, jackals, leopards, and pythons. A female dik-dik hides her newborn offspring to protect it. Only after the youngster is at least 2 weeks old is it strong enough to join its parents and sprint if required. Dik-diks run in an unusual zig-zag pattern when chased. Heavier predators may not be graceful enough to cut back and forth. The dik-dik does well in dry conditions, getting all the water it needs from plants and morning dew.

A scent gland is located below each eye.

The unusual name of this small, shy antelope comes from the sound of its alarm call. When threatened, the animal cries "dik-dik." This cry warns other dik-diks to watch out for danger.

WHERE IN THE WORLD?

Lives mainly in East Africa, from Somalia south through Kenya and Malawi. A western population lives in Angola and Namibia.

HORNS
Only the male has horns, which reach only 4.5 inches (11.4 centimeters) long, with a tuft of longer hair between them.

GLANDS
Dik-diks use secretions from special *glands* (organs) near the eyes to mark their territory.

LEGS
Strong, slender legs help dik-diks to be nimble on their tiny hoofs.

STAYING TOGETHER
Dik-diks pair for life. They occupy the same *territory* (area) and mark the boundaries with dung and scent. The male drives off would-be intruders.

HOW BIG IS IT?

Sable Antelope

SPECIES • *Hippotragus niger*

These animals get their name from the *sable* (black) color of the males. These antelopes often confront *predators* (hunting animals) rather than run away. Their sharp horns can be deadly even to lions.

VITAL STATISTICS

WEIGHT	420–595 lb (190–270 kg)
LENGTH	91–130 in (230–330 cm), including tail
SEXUAL MATURITY	2–3 years; weaned at 8 months
LENGTH OF PREGNANCY	About 279 days; births coincide with the wet season
NUMBER OF OFFSPRING	A single youngster; lies hidden for 10 days after birth
DIET	Eats grasses, leaves, and flowers
LIFESPAN	Up to 17 years in the wild; may reach 20 in captivity

WHERE IN THE WORLD?

Found in southeast Africa, from Kenya to northern South Africa. An isolated population lives in Angola.

ANIMAL FACTS

A single sable antelope bull leads a herd of females and young. Males must fight for control of the herd. They wrestle with their horns, but these are trials of strength, with the forelegs held down on the ground. The males do not usually gore one another with their sharp horns. However, when threatened by a predator, such as a leopard, the sable antelope will aim to cripple its opponent. Young males are forced to leave the herd when they are about 3 years old. A herd that grows too large may split up, providing opportunities for young males to find herds of their own.

Males in combat posture

HORNS
The semicircular horns can reach 66 inches (165 centimeters) in length in mature males. Female horns are somewhat shorter.

COLORATION
Males are predominantly black, while females and young of both sexes are brown.

MANE
This thick area of hair on the neck may protect against attack by lions or leopards, which bite the neck.

UNDERSIDE
The underside of the body is white.

FIGHT NOT FLIGHT
When challenged, sable antelopes can be fierce and determined, often standing their ground rather than running away.

HOW BIG IS IT?

Giant Eland

VITAL STATISTICS

WEIGHT	970–1,984 lb (440–900 kg)
LENGTH	122–150 in (310–380 cm), including tail; up to 72 in (182 cm) tall
SEXUAL MATURITY	Females 15 months–3 years; males 4–5 years
LENGTH OF PREGNANCY	About 279 days; weaning occurs at 6 months
NUMBER OF OFFSPRING	1
DIET	Eats grasses and herbs, as well as taller vegetation
LIFESPAN	Up to 25 years

ANIMAL FACTS

Giant elands live in herds of about 20 individuals, though larger groups have been reported. Mature males live alone for most of the year. Giant elands tend to be so calm by nature that there have been efforts to raise them as livestock. If flushed from cover, they can run away at speeds up to about 42 miles (70 kilometers) per hour. Their numbers have declined in recent years because of hunting and the spread of agriculture. Most giant elands now live in parks and other protected areas.

In spite of their bulk, these elands can jump more than 5 feet (1.5 meters) high.

The description of "giant" for this eland refers to its horns, rather than its overall body size. Its body is not much larger than that of its close relative, the common eland.

WHERE IN THE WORLD?

Found mainly in central Africa, from Cameroon, southern Chad, and the Central African Republic to southwestern Sudan. Also lives in a small area of West Africa.

PATTERNING
A series of parallel grayish-white bands runs down each side of the body from behind the shoulders.

HORNS
Straight and spiralling along their length, the horns can measure up to 48 inches (120 centimeters) long.

DEWLAP
This fold of skin extends down the neck and chest. It is larger in males than females.

HOW BIG IS IT?

EARLY MOMENTS
Giving birth is a dangerous time. But newborns are up and able to walk within minutes.

Oribi

SPECIES • *Ourebia ourebi*

VITAL STATISTICS

WEIGHT	33–46 lb (15–21 kg)
LENGTH	36–55 in (92–140 cm)
SEXUAL MATURITY	Females 10 months; males 14 months
LENGTH OF PREGNANCY	200–215 days
NUMBER OF OFFSPRING	1; weaning occurs after 3.5 months
DIET	Grazes on grass and browses on leaves and shoots
LIFESPAN	Up to 14 years in captivity; shorter in the wild

ANIMAL FACTS

Oribis are solitary or live in pairs. Occasionally, they travel in small groups with up to six members. Their small size makes these animals vulnerable to many predators, including baboons, birds of prey, leopards, and pythons. Often, they rely on *camouflage* (disguise) for protection, freezing in place in tall grass to hide. They also flee from predators, leaping in the air in a movement called *stotting* or *pronking*. The number of oribis has fallen, mostly because of *habitat* (living place) de-struction and *poaching* (illegal hunting).

Only male oribis have horns.

The graceful oribi can disappear into areas of tall grass, enabling it to hide from *predators* (hunting animals). It feeds on grasses and herbs as well as the leaves of bushes and trees.

WHERE IN THE WORLD?

Found in savannas across most of Africa, south of the Sahara.

EYELASHES
Long eyelashes help prevent eye injuries when oribis are in tall grass.

COLORATION
The upper part of the body is orange-brown. The underside is white.

GLANDS
A large, rounded *gland* (organ) below each ear produces scent used to mark *territory* (area).

TAIL
The tail is short and bushy, with a color scheme matching that of the body.

ESCAPING DANGER
Leaping up off the ground is called stotting or pronking. This behavior may confuse a predator, such as this baboon, when it is trying to catch the oribi.

HOW BIG IS IT?

Greater Kudu

The greater kudu is one of the largest and most impressive of all antelopes. It prefers to live in areas of savanna that have bushes and stands of trees, which provide cover.

VITAL STATISTICS

WEIGHT	265–694 lb (120–315 kg); males are heavier
LENGTH	85–118 in (215–300 cm); stands up to 63 in (160 cm) tall
SEXUAL MATURITY	Females 15–21 months; males 21–24 months
LENGTH OF PREGNANCY	Around 279 days
NUMBER OF OFFSPRING	1; weaning at around 180 days
DIET	Eats leaves and shoots; seeks out such fruits as wild watermelons during droughts
LIFESPAN	7–8 years; up to 23 years in captivity

ANIMAL FACTS

The magnificent horns of greater kudus are prized by trophy hunters. As a result, private land owners may keep these animals to earn money. Male kudus are solitary, while females live in small herds with their young. Females lack horns, the longer hair on the throat, and the white chevron. A pregnant female leaves the herd to give birth, and then conceals her offspring in the bush for up to five weeks.

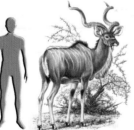

The horns develop with age.

WHERE IN THE WORLD?

Found in eastern and southern parts of Africa, especially from Angola and Namibia across to Zimbabwe and Mozambique. Found north up to Sudan and Ethiopia.

MANE
A line of longer hair extends down the back, with a beard evident on the throat.

HORNS
The male's magnificent spiralling horns can reach up to 60 inches (152 centimeters) long.

CHEVRON
An area of white hair runs between the eyes.

LINEAR PATTERNING
The stripes on the sides of the body break up the animal's outline, providing *camouflage* (disguise).

HOW BIG IS IT?

GETTING CLEAR
After sensing danger, kudus initially freeze, hoping to avoid detection, but they can also run and jump well to escape.

African Buffalo

VITAL STATISTICS

WEIGHT	551–1,984 lb (250–900 kg); males are heavier
LENGTH	87–177 in (220–450 cm)
SEXUAL MATURITY	3.5–5 years
LENGTH OF PREGNANCY	About 340 days; weaning occurs at 6 months
NUMBER OF OFFSPRING	1, rarely 2
DIET	Eats grass, herbs, and swamp vegetation
LIFESPAN	18 years in the wild; up to 29 in captivity

ANIMAL FACTS

African buffaloes may live in savannas or forests. Those living in forests have shorter horns and smaller bodies. Females and their offspring live in large herds. Males usually live in small groups. Like many other African animals, these buffaloes typically *migrate* (move from place to place) with the rains, seeking abundant grass. The *species* (kind) suffered a dramatic decline because of the disease rinderpest, which has been eliminated from the wild. Other threats include hunting and *habitat* (living place) destruction. Today, the population is healthy, though African buffaloes survive mainly in protected areas.

The area of horn over the head is described as the boss.

The mighty African buffalo has a fearsome reputation, with reports of bulls charging and trampling people. Scientists have found that bulls wounded by hunters account for most of these attacks.

WHERE IN THE WORLD?

Lives in much of Africa south of the Sahara, mostly in protected areas.

HORNS
Particularly large in males, the horns can grow up to 63 inches (160 centimeters) long.

COLORATION
This varies from black in male plains buffaloes to red in forest buffaloes.

BODY SHAPE
The wide chest and muscular, barrel-shaped body reflect the power of these buffaloes.

GETTING THE ITCH
Scratching on a tree trunk may ease irritation caused by ticks, which are often removed from the buffalo's body by birds called oxpeckers.

HOW BIG IS IT?

Blue Wildebeest

VITAL STATISTICS

WEIGHT	309–638 lb (140–290 kg)
LENGTH	91–134 in (230–340 cm), including tail
SEXUAL MATURITY	Females 1.5–2.5 years; males 3–4 years
LENGTH OF PREGNANCY	248–262 days
NUMBER OF OFFSPRING	A single youngster, typically weaned by 4 months
DIET	Grazes on grass
LIFESPAN	15–20 years maximum

ANIMAL FACTS

Despite their name, some blue wildebeests are brownish-gray. These animals face many predators, including cheetahs, hyenas, lions, and wild dogs. A herd confronts a predator by bunching together, stamping, and making loud calls. The young are on their feet and walking within 15 minutes of birth. Mothers defend their calves, often driving off cheetahs and hyenas.

Blue wildebeest

Black wildebeest

Wildebeests are famous for their long *migration* (travel) to reach abundant grass. More than 1 million of these animals cross the savanna, braving crocodile-infested rivers and a host of other *predators* (hunters).

WHERE IN THE WORLD?

Found in various parts of East Africa, from Kenya down to northern South Africa, and east to Angola and eastern Namibia.

HORNS
Horns are longer in males, measuring up to 33 inches (83 centimeters) long.

BANDING
These barred markings can be mistaken for wrinkles in the skin from a distance.

TAIL
The hair in the tail is black and very long, similar to that of a horse.

A CALF
All young blue wildebeests are tawny-brown at first; their color changes beginning at about two months.

HOW BIG IS IT?

MASS BIRTHING
Young are born all together, about two weeks before the rains arrive. This overwhelms predators and means there is plenty of fresh grass.

Common Zebra

SPECIES • *Equus burchelli*

Zebra stripes may confuse biting insects or make it difficult for *predators* (hunting animals) to pick out an individual from the herd, especially in low light. The stripes may also help zebras recognize each other.

VITAL STATISTICS

WEIGHT	About 770 lb (350 kg); males are larger
LENGTH	8.2 ft (2.5 m); up to 55 in (140 cm) tall at the shoulder
SEXUAL MATURITY	2–4 years
LENGTH OF PREGNANCY	12–13 months
NUMBER OF OFFSPRING	1; weaning occurs at about 12 months
DIET	Grazes on grasses and other low-growing plants
LIFESPAN	20–25 years; up to 40 in captivity

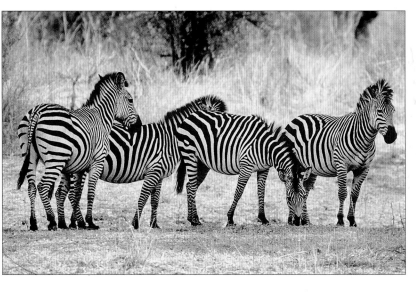

WHERE IN THE WORLD?

Lives in eastern Africa, from parts of South Sudan and Ethiopia south through Uganda, Kenya, Tanzania, Zambia and Zimbabwe, to Angola, Botswana, and northern South Africa.

ANIMAL FACTS

Zebras live in family groups of several females and their offspring, led by a single male. Zebras often gather with other creatures of the plains, such as wildebeests and ostriches. When faced with predators, the zebra makes a high-pitched alarm call. Females protect their offspring, while the male defends his *harem* (group of females) with powerful kicks and bites. During the night, at least one member of the harem remains awake at all times, to keep an eye out for lions and other predators.

The facial patterning of each zebra is also unique.

SHADOW STRIPING
The skin of a zebra is actually black. The stripes are usually white, though they may also be brown or gray.

MANE
The mane stands upright, with the striped patterning extending through the hair.

LEG STRIPES
The leg stripes fade out, especially among zebras in southern Africa.

DEFENDING THEMSELVES
Zebras may appear defenseless against such predators as hyenas, but a well-struck blow from their hind feet can be fatal.

HOW BIG IS IT?

Giraffe

VITAL STATISTICS

WEIGHT	Females 2,425–3,525 lb (1,100–1,600 kg); males 2,865–4,410 lb (1,300–2,000 kg)
LENGTH	180–225 in (457–570 cm), including tail
SEXUAL MATURITY	3–5 years
LENGTH OF PREGNANCY	434–465 days; weaning occurs 12–16 months later
NUMBER OF OFFSPRING	1, standing 72 in (180 cm) tall at birth
DIET	Browses at high level, particularly on the leaves of mimosa and acacia trees
LIFESPAN	20–25 years; up to 28 in captivity

ANIMAL FACTS

The giraffe's unusual height enables it to reach the leaves of tall trees. It plucks away the leaves using its long lips and tongue, which can be as long as about 21 inches (53 centimeters). The long neck of a giraffe requires a strong heart, to supply the brain with blood. In fact, a giraffe's heart weighs up to 22 pounds (10 kilograms) and measures around 2 feet (61 centimeters) long. Lions are the only major *predators* (hunters) of adult giraffes, though kicks from the giraffe's powerful legs can kill a lion. The giraffe's closest living relatives are the okapi and the pronghorn.

The giraffe is the tallest living *species* (kind) of animal on Earth, standing more than 18 feet (5.5 meters) tall. Their height enables these animals to reach the leaves of such tall trees as acacias.

WHERE IN THE WORLD?

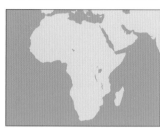

Found in much of Africa south of the Sahara, particularly in eastern and southern parts.

GUARDIANS
The keen eyesight and height of giraffes enable them to spot danger from afar. They often alert other animals to the presence of predators.

APPEARANCE
The patterns on the hide differ among individuals and among populations in different areas.

HORNS
The "horns" are covered by skin and hair. They are not true horns.

NECK STRUCTURE
Despite its length, the giraffe's neck has just as many bones as the necks of other mammals. The neck bones are simply longer.

HOW BIG IS IT?

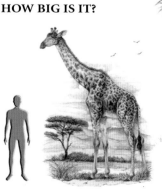

LOWER DOWN
Despite their height, giraffes occasionally sit down, but getting back up can be slow and awkward.

White Rhinoceros

SPECIES • *Ceratotherium simum*

VITAL STATISTICS

WEIGHT	4,000–6,000 lb (1,800–2,700 kg); males are bigger
LENGTH	10.8–13.8 ft (3.3–4.2 m); up to 73 in (185 cm) tall at the shoulder
SEXUAL MATURITY	Females 6–7 years; males 10–12 years
LENGTH OF PREGNANCY	16–18 months
NUMBER OF OFFSPRING	1; weaning occurs at about 12 months
DIET	Grazes on grasses and other low-growing plants
LIFESPAN	Up to 45 years

The white rhinoceros is targeted by *poachers* (illegal hunters) for its large horn, which is used in traditional Chinese medicine. Some populations of rhinos have already been wiped out in the wild.

WHERE IN THE WORLD?

Now found only in Kenya, Uganda, Zimbabwe, and South Africa. A northern population once lived in southern Chad, the Central African Republic, South Sudan, and the Democratic Republic of the Congo.

ANIMAL FACTS

Southern white rhinos were nearly wiped out by hunting by the year 1900. Since then, protection in parks has helped them to recover, though they remain threatened by poachers. The northern white rhino, which some scientists consider a separate species, has been hunted to *extinction* (death) in the wild. White rhinos are not white. Their name is a garbled translation of an African word meaning *wide,* which refers to their wide mouth.

Rhinoceroses have small eyes and poor vision, but their large ears provide keen hearing.

HORNS
There are two horns, with the front horn being longer.

COLORATION
The skin of these rhinoceroses is gray, and they have virtually no hair.

MOUTH
This species is also known as the wide-lipped or square-lipped rhinoceros because of the shape of its mouth.

TOES
These rhinos have three toes on each foot.

HOW BIG IS IT?

MUD PUPPIES

Rhinoceroses *wallow* (roll about) regularly in mud. This behavior helps them to cool off, and the mud protects their skin from biting insects.

African Elephant

The African elephant is Earth's largest living land animal. Although conservation efforts provide some protection for these magnificent animals, they remain threatened by habitat destruction and poaching.

VITAL STATISTICS

WEIGHT	5,000–14,000 lb (2,270–6,350 kg); males are larger
LENGTH	9.2–11.2 ft (2.8–3.4 m); up to 13 ft (4 m) tall at the shoulder
SEXUAL MATURITY	Females 10–11 years; males 10–20 years
LENGTH OF PREGNANCY	Around 22 months, the longest of any mammal
NUMBER OF OFFSPRING	1; weaning occurs at 6.5 years; females give birth every 4 years
DIET	Feeds on a variety of plant matter
LIFESPAN	Up to 70 years

ANIMAL FACTS

Elephants roam over large areas, in herds led by a senior female who knows the territory well and can remember the locations of waterholes in times of drought. Herds consist of females and their young. Mature male elephants, called bulls, live alone. Elephants have huge appetites, with adults able to eat 300 pounds (136 kilograms) of food daily. Elephants can communicate through *infrasound*, which is too low-pitched to be heard by people.

African elephants (above, left) have four or five toes on their front feet and three in back. Asian elephants (above, right) have five toes in front and four in back.

WHERE IN THE WORLD?

Scattered throughout much of Africa, in areas south of the Sahara.

TRUNK
Controlled by 100,000 muscles, the trunk is sensitive enough to pick up small objects.

TUSKS
These modified teeth, made of ivory, can grow to a length of 8 feet (2.4 meters) and weigh up to 100 pounds (45 kilograms).

EARS
These help the elephant to keep cool by giving off body heat.

SKIN
The rough skin has a thick, leathery texture.

MOTHERHOOD

Herd members are very protective toward their young, and females will challenge such *predators* (hunting animals) as lions that attack young elephants.

HOW BIG IS IT?

Spotted Hyena

The cackling calls made by this animal sound like giggling, which is why it is also known as the "laughing hyena." Although it is sometimes described as a scavenger, the hyena hunts most of its prey.

VITAL STATISTICS

WEIGHT	99–154 lb (45–70 kg); females are slightly bigger
LENGTH	35–60 in (95–150 cm), including tail; up to 30 in (75 cm) tall
SEXUAL MATURITY	About 3 years
LENGTH OF PREGNANCY	77 days
NUMBER OF OFFSPRING	2; weaning occurs at 14–18 months
DIET	Hunts a variety of prey, including wildebeests, zebras, and smaller prey; also *scavenges* (feeds on animal remains)
LIFESPAN	10–12 years in the wild; up to 25 in captivity

WHERE IN THE WORLD?

Lives throughout Africa, south of the Sahara.

ANIMAL FACTS

Spotted hyenas are fearsome *predators* (hunting animals) that work together to take down large prey. They compete for food with lions, which often attack hyenas. Hyenas live in groups called clans, which are ruled by females. Hyena mothers hide their newborns in *burrows* (underground shelters) before moving them to a larger den. Spotted hyena milk is rich, enabling young to go days without suckling. Despite their appearance, hyenas are more closely related to cats than to dogs.

Hyenas are able to bite through bone.

HEAD AND JAWS
Strong jaws are supported by a thick neck with a mane of longer fur.

APPEARANCE
The coat has a rough texture and individual spotted patterning. The background color tends to fade with age.

PROFILE
Hyenas have a distinctive hunchbacked appearance, with the body sloping down to the hindquarters.

SCENT-MARKING
Hyenas produce a yellow, oily substance, which they use to mark their *territory* (area).

HOW BIG IS IT?

Cheetah

VITAL STATISTICS

WEIGHT	77–143 lb (35–65 kg)
LENGTH	72–90 in (183–229 cm); about 35 in (90 cm) tall
SEXUAL MATURITY	Females 1–2 years; males about 1 year
LENGTH OF PREGNANCY	90–98 days
NUMBER OF OFFSPRING	Averages 3–5, but can be up to 9; weaning occurs at around 90 days
DIET	Feeds on gazelles and a variety of small animals
LIFESPAN	1–12 years in the wild; up to 20 in captivity

ANIMAL FACTS

The cheetah can go from a dead stop to a speed of 40 miles (64 kilometers) per hour in just three strides. But if it has not caught its prey in just 600 yards (550 meters), the cheetah must slow down again. The cheetah knocks down prey and grabs it by the throat. It eats quickly because lions or hyenas may steal the meal. Females live alone except when they have young. Males form small groups.

The cheetah is the fastest land animal on Earth over short distances, reaching speeds of 50 to 70 miles (80 to 110 kilometers) per hour. The number of cheetahs has fallen dramatically.

WHERE IN THE WORLD?

Now mainly found in southern and eastern Africa, especially in Namibia, Botswana, Kenya, and Tanzania. Rare in northern Africa. Nearly eliminated from Asia.

EYES
The cheetah relies on its sharp eyesight to spot prey. It hunts during the day.

PATTERNING
No two cheetahs have identical patterning. The spots can be up to 2 inches (5 centimeters) in diameter.

COLORATION
Color can vary from tan to buff. The underside of the body is white.

TAIL
The spots on the tail run together to create rings.

HOW BIG IS IT?

STRETCHING AHEAD

The stride of a cheetah is about the same length as that of a horse, even though the cheetah's body is shorter. The cheetah's back acts like a spring, propelling it forward and enabling it to cover 20 to 25 feet (6 to 7.6 meters) in a single bound.

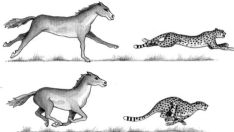

Lion

VITAL STATISTICS

WEIGHT	330–550 lb (150–250 kg)
LENGTH	102–141 in (260–360 cm)
SEXUAL MATURITY	3–4 years
LENGTH OF PREGNANCY	100–119 days
NUMBER OF OFFSPRING	1–6
DIET	Usually larger mammals, especially wildebeest, buffalo, and zebra
LIFESPAN	7–10 years; up to 30 in captivity

Unlike other cats, lions live in groups. Known as prides, these groups are usually made up of 10 to 20 lions, though they may have 40. Males are larger and stronger than females, which are called lionesses.

WHERE IN THE WORLD?

Now restricted to Africa south of the Sahara, particularly on the eastern side of the continent. A small population survives in the Gir Forest, in India.

ANIMAL FACTS

Lions usually hunt at night. They cannot out-run most prey, so they rely on stealth and am-bush. Lionesses do most of the hunting and often work together. For example, lionesses may hide in the grass while others drive prey toward them. Male lions have short lives, for they must fight other males for their place in the pride. They drive off male cubs when the cubs are 2 or 3 years old. In time, the young lions will fight to take over a pride. Lions once lived in Europe and the Middle East, but people killed them all. Only a few hundred survive in one area of India. The lion's numbers have also fallen in Africa, mainly because people have killed them.

If a new male takes over a pride, he may kill the cubs, ensuring that only his cubs will be raised by the pride.

MANE
Only mature male lions have this long area of hair surrounding the face and extending on to the chest.

EYES
Lions have keen eyesight to spot prey *camouflaged* (disguised) to blend in with the grass.

COLORATION
The mane tends to darken with age, often ending up predominantly black in older individuals.

TAIL
The fur on a lion's body is relatively short, though the tail ends in a dark tip of longer hair.

HOW BIG IS IT?

PRIDE AT STAKE
Males fight over the right to lead a pride. Their manes help to protect them from claws.

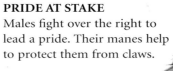

Serval

VITAL STATISTICS

WEIGHT	18–40 lb (8–18 kg)
LENGTH	36–57 in (91–145 cm), including tail; up to 26 in (65 cm) tall
SEXUAL MATURITY	12–24 months
LENGTH OF PREGNANCY	66–77 days
NUMBER OF OFFSPRING	Average 1–3, but can be up to 5; weaning occurs at 120–180 days
DIET	Hunts small mammals, especially rodents; some fish, frogs, and birds
LIFESPAN	Average 10–12 years, but can be up to 20

ANIMAL FACTS

The serval is a skilled *predator* (hunter) of small animals. In fact, one of every two attempts ends in a kill, a higher success rate than that of other wild cats. However, the serval is a relatively large cat that feeds on small prey, so it must catch many animals. After it detects prey, the serval slinks forward and leaps up to 13 feet (4 meters), pinning prey with its front paws. Serval kittens may allow prey to scurry away only to pounce once again. This behavior gives kittens practice in seizing prey.

The backs of the ears have distinctive markings.

The serval relies on its keen hearing to hunt small animals, especially rodents. It remains motionless for up to 15 minutes as it listens for prey. If the serval detects prey, it approaches in silence and pounces.

WHERE IN THE WORLD?

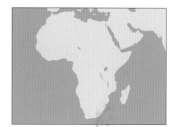

Lives widely south of the Sahara, outside the central rain forest region and southern parts of Africa. Now almost *extinct* (wiped out) in north-western Africa.

TAIL
The tail is short in relation to the legs. It ends in a dark tip.

LEGS
Servals are taller than any other wild cat, in relation to their body size.

HEAD
The head is relatively small. Servals have large ears and a long neck.

SPOTS
The spots are black and often quite large, joining to form stripes over the back.

NO ESCAPE
Servals can also hear rodents hiding in *burrows* (underground dwellings). They can quickly dig out this prey to feed on it.

HOW BIG IS IT?

Meerkat

VITAL STATISTICS

WEIGHT	1.3–2.1 lb (0.62–0.97 kg)
LENGTH	31–36 in (80–91 cm), including tail; up to 12 in (30 cm) tall
SEXUAL MATURITY	12 months
LENGTH OF PREGNANCY	77 days
NUMBER OF OFFSPRING	1–5; weaning at 49–63 days
DIET	Eats mainly spiders and insects; also eats some eggs and lizards, plus plant matter
LIFESPAN	7–10 in the wild; up to 12 in captivity

ANIMAL FACTS

The burrow is so important to meerkat survival that these animals are only common in areas with firm soil, which can support tunnels. The members of the group each take turns watching for danger rather than *foraging* (searching) for food. They stand for a better view, scanning for threats. Hawks and other birds of prey are especially dangerous. If a hawk approaches, the meerkat on guard duty gives an alarm call. The meerkats then run for the nearest entrance to their burrow.

Strong, curved claws are great for digging.

Meerkats are highly social, living in packs with up to 30 members. They live in complex *burrows* (underground shelters) with many entrances. When danger nears, the meerkats give a cry and scurry inside.

WHERE IN THE WORLD?

Restricted to southern and southwestern Africa, ranging from Angola and Namibia into Botswana and South Africa.

EYES
The eyes are large and set high in the skull, giving excellent eyesight.

HEAD
The skull is domed, with a pointed muzzle. The small ears are located at the sides of the head.

UNDERSIDE
The underside is a lighter shade of gray than the back.

STANDING TALL
Meerkats stand up when watching for danger.

HOW BIG IS IT?

POWERFUL BITE
The meerkat's sharp teeth can crack the tough body casings of insect prey.

Cape Porcupine

The Cape porcupine is the largest rodent in Africa. If attacked, porcupines defend themselves by striking enemies with their quilled tails. Porcupines cannot shoot the quills at their enemies.

VITAL STATISTICS

WEIGHT	40–66 lb (18–30 kg); females slightly heavier
LENGTH	29–34 in (74–87 cm); tail is 1 in (2.5 cm)
SEXUAL MATURITY	Females 9–16 months; males 8–18 months
LENGTH OF PREGNANCY	About 135 days; 2 litters a year
NUMBER OF OFFSPRING	1–4; weaning occurs at 100 days
DIET	Mainly fruits and other plant matter; also scavenges on animal remains
LIFESPAN	12–15 years

ANIMAL FACTS

Cape porcupines spend the day resting in *burrows* (underground dwellings), which may extend to 66 feet (20 meters) of tunnel that opens into a large chamber. At night, they come out to eat fruit and dig for tubers and roots. These rodents are usually solitary, though pairs with young have been spotted. The young are born with soft spines and quills, but these soon harden in the air. The spines over the tail are hollow. When threatened, the animal shakes these spines to make a rattling sound. This sound warns predators to keep their distance.

Quills and spines lost in a fight grow back quickly.

WHERE IN THE WORLD?

Lives in central and southern Africa, except for the Namib Desert in the southwest.

HEAD
The head is covered in short hairs, with whiskers that help the rodent to feel its surroundings in the dark.

SPINES
Spines and quills are both long, sharp bristles of hairs that are *fused* (grown together). Spines are thicker and longer, reaching 20 inches (50 centimeters).

QUILLS
These are shorter and less prominent than spines, growing to about 12 inches (30 centimeters) in length.

HOW BIG IS IT?

DEFENSE TACTICS
A *predator* (hunting animal) that attacks a porcupine runs a real risk of getting a face full of spines and quills.

Aardvark

VITAL STATISTICS

WEIGHT	88–143 lb (40–65 kg)
LENGTH	4.5–6.5 ft (1.4–2 m)
SEXUAL MATURITY	Around 2 years
LENGTH OF PREGNANCY	About 7 months
NUMBER OF OFFSPRING	1; weaning occurs after about 4 months
DIET	Termites and ants, using a tongue measuring up to 12 in (30 cm) long
LIFESPAN	Around 10 years; up to 23 in captivity

ANIMAL FACTS

The aardvark's appetite is huge. It can consume up to 50,000 ants in a single night. With its powerful front claws, the aardvark rips the nest apart. The aardvark probes with its long, sticky tongue, drawing insects into its mouth. The bites of ants seem to have no effect on aardvarks. Aardvarks also use their claws to create *burrows* (underground dwellings). These burrows can have up to eight entrances and may extend up to 43 feet (13 meters) underground. Many other animals use abandoned aardvark burrows, including hyenas, reptiles, squirrels, and warthogs. Aardvarks usually live alone, except for mothers with young. They are active at night. They have poor eyesight but sharp hearing and smell.

The name of this unusual mammal comes from words in Afrikaans that mean *earth pig*. However, aardvarks are not closely related to pigs.

WHERE IN THE WORLD?

Found across much of Africa below the Sahara, but not in west-central parts or the Horn of Africa (northeastern Africa).

EARS
Tall yet slender, the ears can move independently to listen for *predators* (hunting animals), especially when the aardvark is feeding.

FOOT FALL
The front feet (top) have four toes, while hind feet (bottom) have five toes.

TAIL
This is largely hairless and hangs down. It is broad at its base and tapers to the tip.

SNOUT
The snout has a disk-like structure at the tip, where the nostrils are located. The mouth is small.

DEFENSIVE STRATEGY
If cornered, the aardvark rolls over to protect its neck and lashes out with the claws on its feet.

HOW BIG IS IT?

Springhare

The springhare resembles a miniature kangaroo, with short arms and powerful legs. Despite its name, the springhare is a rodent, not a *hare* (an animal related to but larger than rabbits).

VITAL STATISTICS

WEIGHT	6.6–8.8 lb (3–4 kg)
LENGTH	28–37 in (71–94 cm) overall; tail is the same length as the body
SEXUAL MATURITY	About 2¾ years
LENGTH OF PREGNANCY	About 80 days; up to 3 litters a year
NUMBER OF OFFSPRING	1; weaning occurs at 49 days
DIET	Eats such crops as wheat, oats, and barley, plus beetles, grasshoppers, and other insects
LIFESPAN	8–14 years

ANIMAL FACTS

Living in relatively open country, these rodents rely on their ability to jump in order to evade *predators* (hunting animals). They live in their *burrows* (underground dwellings) during the day. At dusk, they come out to feed. Their large ears and eyes provide excellent hearing and eyesight. Their ears are protected by a tuft of hair to prevent sand from entering the ear canal when they are digging. People have long hunted springhares using a pole with a barb, which they stab into the burrow.

Springhares jump on their hind legs, like kangaroos.

WHERE IN THE WORLD?

Lives in southeastern and southern parts of Africa, in Kenya, Tanzania, the Democratic Republic of the Congo, Angola, Zambia, Zimbabwe, Botswana, Mozambique, Namibia, and South Africa.

MATERNAL BOND
Springhares produce only one offspring at a time, which they raise with care.

NECK
Short and muscular, the neck supports the weight of the head.

TAIL
The long tail helps the springhare maintain its balance.

COLORATION
This is variable, ranging from reddish-brown to a dull gray. The underside is white.

HIND FEET
These are much longer than the front feet, each having four toes with strong claws.

HIDING AWAY
If it detects danger, a springhare flees to its burrow and seals itself inside by creating a soil barrier.

HOW BIG IS IT?

Griffon Vulture

VITAL STATISTICS

WEIGHT	13–28.5 lb (6–13 kg)
LENGTH	37.4–43.3 in (95–110 cm)
WINGSPAN	7.5–8.7 ft (230–265 cm)
INCUBATION PERIOD	51–53 days
NUMBER OF BROODS	1 a year
TYPICAL DIET	Scavenges on animal remains, especially those of large animals, such as goats and sheep
LIFESPAN	Up to 55 years

The majestic griffon vulture soars high above the ground, relying on its excellent eyesight to spot the animal remains on which it feeds. Like many other European birds, it flies to Africa in the winter.

WHERE IN THE WORLD?

Migrates (travels) to northern Africa, to areas south of the Sahara, from isolated pockets in southern Europe. Also lives in southwestern Asia.

ANIMAL FACTS

The griffon vulture often forms large flocks and nests in colonies, with up to 100 pairs of birds building nests on cliff faces. The vulture prefers open spaces, where it can survey large areas for *carrion* (dead and decaying animal flesh). Many vultures may gather and compete for a chance to feed on the body. The griffon vulture was once common in Europe, but today it survives only in pockets. People have shot and poisoned many of these birds. However, their numbers have begun to recover after decades of legal protection.

BILL
The bill is large and powerful, with a hooked tip to tear open the hides of dead animals.

WINGS
The wide wings are used to soar on *thermals* (rising air currents), enabling the vulture to remain aloft for long periods.

FEET
The legs are short and the feet are large. The bird often hops along the ground instead of walking.

Griffon vultures in flight

HOW BIG IS IT?

CLEANING SERVICE

Vultures provide an important service by *scavenging* (eating animal remains), which helps to prevent the spread of disease and limits the numbers of such pests as rats, which also feed on carrion.

Long-Crested Eagle

SPECIES • *Lophaetus occipitalis*

VITAL STATISTICS

LENGTH	21–23 in (53–58 cm)
WINGSPAN	4–5 ft (1.2–1.5 m)
NUMBER OF EGGS	1–2
INCUBATION PERIOD	40–43 days
NUMBER OF BROODS	1 a year
TYPICAL DIET	Feeds on rodents, especially rats, as well as shrews, birds, reptiles, and large insects
LIFESPAN	15–20 years

The elegant long-crested eagle is named for the crown of feathers on top of its head. The crest may be important in attracting mates.

WHERE IN THE WORLD?

Widely distributed in Africa south of the Sahara, though it is absent from the Horn of Africa (northeast Africa) and much of South Africa, where it is found only in coastal areas.

ANIMAL FACTS

The long-crested eagle is found in wooded savannas, especially near rivers and wetlands. It favors areas with trees partly because it prefers to perch rather than soar as it searches for prey. After it spots prey, the eagle swoops down and clutches the animal in its sharp *talons* (claws). It then carries the prey back to its perch to feed. It is relatively small for a bird of prey. Its small size and relatively large wings make it graceful in flight, enabling it to catch small birds.

These eagles perch and watch for rodent prey.

HEAD
The long crest of feathers on the head is raised when the bird is perching but kept flat during flight.

WINGS
The wings help this small eagle swoop quickly and easily onto its prey, enabling it to catch such small, agile creatures as rodents and reptiles.

EAGLE VOCABULARY

Young eagles are called *eaglets* or *eyasses*. The soft, fluffy feathers on an eaglet is called *down*. The nests of eagles sometimes are called aeries or eyries (pronounced *AIR eez* or *IHR eez*).

TAIL
The wide tail has three distinctive pale bars, which can be used to identify the bird during flight.

HOW BIG IS IT?

RENDING THE FLESH

The short, powerful bill is curved with a hook at the tip. This shape helps the bird to pierce flesh and tear away hunks.

Bateleur Eagle

Africa's snake-eating eagles are named after French tightrope walkers, because they tend to tip the ends of their wings while flying, much like a tightrope walker uses a pole for balance.

VITAL STATISTICS

LENGTH	22–24 in (56–61 cm)
WINGSPAN	5.7 ft (1.7 m)
SEXUAL MATURITY	7 years
INCUBATION PERIOD	52–60 days
FLEDGLING PERIOD	93–194 days
NUMBER OF EGGS	1 egg
NUMBER OF BROODS	1 a year
HABITS	Active at day
TYPICAL DIET	Feeds on snakes and other reptiles, birds, mammals, insects, and animal remains
LIFESPAN	Up to 23 years

ANIMAL FACTS

Bateleur (pronounced *bat LERR*) eagles are capable of impressive mid-air acrobatics, which males use to impress females. They nest in the canopies of large trees. The chicks are not strong enough to leave the nest for 110 days. Even then, they return for food for another 100 days. Even with all this care, only a small number survive to adulthood. These birds have declined in numbers, mostly because of poisoning and destruction of their *habitat* (kind of place in which an animal lives).

Juvenile

WHERE IN THE WORLD?

Found throughout much of sub-Saharan Africa, in areas of open savanna with tall trees available for nests.

WINGS
The gray, inner layer of secondary feathers on the wings identifies this bird as a female.

FEATHERED ARMOUR
When attacking a snake, the eagle fluffs up its feathers for protection. If the snake strikes, it gets only a mouthful of feathers.

TAIL
These eagles have an unusually short tail. The short tail reduces *drag* (force working against a body in flight) and helps the eagle to soar for long periods.

FACIAL COLOR
This can vary from pale to brilliant red, depending on the mood of the bird. Males often display red faces during the breeding season.

HOW BIG IS IT?

FLIGHT CONTROLS
To provide additional lift in the air, bateleur eagles have more secondary feathers at the back of the wings than do most other birds of prey. Long, fingerlike primary feathers at the ends of the wings give additional control.

Eurasian Hobby

VITAL STATISTICS

WEIGHT	4.6–8 oz (130–230 g)
LENGTH	12.2–14.2 in (31–36 cm)
WINGSPAN	25.6–33 in (70–84 cm)
NUMBER OF EGGS	2–3 eggs
INCUBATION PERIOD	28–31 days
NUMBER OF BROODS	1 a year
TYPICAL DIET	Feeds on small birds and large flying insects, especially dragonflies
LIFESPAN	Up to 15 years

The small, elegant Eurasian hobby is fast and graceful enough to be able to catch highly maneuverable swifts in the air. It also catches dragonflies, transferring the insects from *talons* (claws) to bill as it soars.

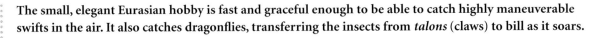

WHERE IN THE WORLD?

Migrates (travels) to the savannas of central and southern Africa during the winter. Summers in most of Europe, across Asia to the Pacific Ocean.

ANIMAL FACTS

The Eurasian hobby is a type of falcon. Like other falcons, it is extremely graceful and swift in flight. In fact, falcons are the fastest of all animals, reaching up to 200 miles (322 kilometers) per hour in dives. It is such a threat to small birds that some birds have special alarm calls used only to identify the hobby. During the breeding season, the hobby tends to occupy the old nests of other birds, especially crows. The female usually *incubates* (cares for) the eggs, while the male does most of the hunting. The bird has been used in falconry, in which a bird of prey is trained to obey commands and hunt *game* (wild animals).

The Eurasian hobby has distinctive facial patterning.

WINGS
The wings are long and streamlined for very fast and maneuverable flight.

TAIL
The tail is long and wide. It is important for maneuvering when the *raptor* (bird of prey) is in high-speed pursuit of prey.

FEET
The large yellow feet have powerful toes armed with sharp, black talons for seizing prey.

HOW BIG IS IT?

A DEADLY VISITOR
The Eurasian hobby winters in sub-Saharan Africa, where the birds often take advantage of the abundance of flying termites when these large insects come out to breed.

Martial Eagle

VITAL STATISTICS

WEIGHT	14.3 lb (6.5 kg)
LENGTH	30.7–33.8 in (78–86 cm)
WINGSPAN	8.2 ft (2.5 m)
SEXUAL MATURITY	5–6 years
INCUBATION PERIOD	47–53 days
FLEDGLING PERIOD	59–99 days
NUMBER OF EGGS	1 egg every 2 years
HABITS	Active at day
TYPICAL DIET	Relatively small mammals, birds, and reptiles
LIFESPAN	Typically 16 years

ANIMAL FACTS

The martial eagle soars high above the ground. When it spots prey, it plunges and strikes with its sharp *talons* (claws). Although it sometimes attacks small antelopes, this eagle more often hunts *hares* (animals related to rabbits) and rodents. It also may attack baboons and other monkeys. The eagles are thought to mate for life. They build their nests in large trees. A nest is 4 to 6 feet (1.2 to 1.8 meters) across. It is made of sticks and lined with green leaves. The numbers of these birds have fallen, mainly because people have shot and poisoned them.

Juveniles are gray, with white below.

These magnificent birds of prey are Africa's largest eagle. They are powerful enough to kill and carry away a small antelope.

WHERE IN THE WORLD?

Found across sub-Saharan Africa, especially Zimbabwe and South Africa. They are rare in central Africa and other heavily forested areas.

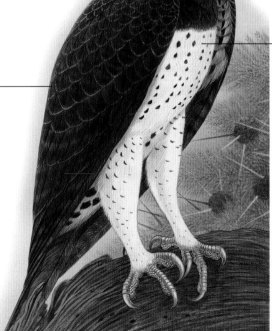

EYES
Like other *raptors* (birds of prey), these birds have extremely good eyesight, enabling them to spot prey from high up in the air.

SPECKLES
As a general rule, older birds have more speckles and darker feathers.

WINGS
Large, broad wings are the ideal design for soaring, while finger-like primary feathers give greater control in the air.

HOW BIG IS IT?

DEATH GRIP

Like many raptors, martial eagles use their sharp talons to hold down and kill their prey. Holding their claws outstretched while in flight, they can grab even quickly moving prey with relative ease.

Helmeted Guineafowl

SPECIES • *Numida meleagris*

VITAL STATISTICS

WEIGHT	3 lb (1.3 kg)
LENGTH	17–19 in (42.5–48 cm)
SEXUAL MATURITY	Around 2 years
LAYS EGGS	Just after the rainy season
INCUBATION PERIOD	26–28 days
FLEDGLING PERIOD	Around 70 days
NUMBER OF EGGS	20–30 eggs, but up to 50 are recorded
CALL	A stuttering 'keerrrr' sound
TYPICAL DIET	Seeds, roots, insects, small amphibians, mammals, and reptiles
LIFESPAN	Up to 15 years

ANIMAL FACTS

Guineafowl are related to such birds as pheasants and turkeys, and they have a similar way of life. They feed on the ground in flocks of 20 or more. They also build their nests on the ground, hiding them in grass or other vegetation. Guineafowl benefit people by eating large numbers of ticks, which might otherwise spread disease. People also raise these birds for their eggs and meat.

Unlike pheasants and turkeys, male and female guineafowl look much alike.

Guineafowl spend most of their time walking on the ground, searching for food. They usually fly only a short distance, to escape from danger.

WHERE IN THE WORLD?

Widely distributed in Africa south of the Sahara, except for dense forests and deserts. Farmed in parts of Europe and the United States.

WINGS
Guineafowl have short, broad wings. If threatened, they may launch into the air and then glide a short distance.

HEAD
Male guineafowl have a larger *helmet* (large bony lump atop the head) and *wattles* (fleshy patches on the cheeks) than do females.

LEGS
Males fight over territory and mates with their legs, sometimes causing serious injury with their claws.

HOW BIG IS IT?

POWER WALKERS, POWER SQUAWKERS

These birds can walk up to 6 miles (10 kilometers) a day in search of food. Their continual harsh cries make them unpopular, though they serve as good "watchdogs."

African Stonechat

SPECIES • *Saxicola torquatus*

VITAL STATISTICS

WEIGHT	0.5 oz (15 g)
LENGTH	About 5 in (13 cm)
WINGSPAN	9 in (23 cm)
NUMBER OF EGGS	5–6 eggs
INCUBATION PERIOD	14–15 days
NUMBER OF BROODS	2 a year
TYPICAL DIET	Insects, worms, and spiders
LIFESPAN	Up to 7 years

The African stonechat is a small bird that perches on plant stems or fence posts. It makes a call that sounds like two stones being struck together.

WHERE IN THE WORLD?

Found in Africa, south of the Sahara. Most common in southern Africa, but extends west to Côte d'Ivoire, north to Sudan, and east to Madagascar.

ANIMAL FACTS

The African stonechat usually swoops down from its perch onto insects on the ground. But it is so graceful in flight that it can also catch insects in mid-air, a behavior known as "hawking." The bird can also hover in place. The female stonechat builds the nest, often on the ground but sometimes in a small tree. The nest is made of dry grass or plant stems and is lined with hair and feathers. The female *incubates* (cares for) the eggs, but both parents bring the hatched chicks food. Stonechats are sometimes victims of cuckoos, which sneak their own eggs into the nest. The young cuckoos kill the stonechat chicks and trick the parents into feeding them.

WINGS
The wings are relatively short, with long primary feathers at the tips. These suit a bird that must maneuver to catch flying insects but rarely flies far.

TAIL
The broad tail helps the stonechat to change direction while flying.

BILL
The bill is short but relatively wide, which helps the bird to snatch insect prey.

The male stonechat in flight

HOW BIG IS IT?

HUNGRY MOUTHS TO FEED
The female builds a nest of dry grass and plant stems and lines it with hair and feathers. She lays five to six eggs. When the eggs hatch, both the male and female bring the chicks food.

Sudan Golden Sparrow

SPECIES • *Passer luteus*

VITAL STATISTICS

LENGTH	4–5 in (10–13 cm)
SEXUAL MATURITY	2 years
INCUBATION PERIOD	1–12 days
FLEDGLING PERIOD	13–14 days
NUMBER OF EGGS	2–6 eggs
NUMBER OF BROODS	1; occasionally 2–3 a year
CALL	Chirrup
HABITS	Active at day
TYPICAL DIET	Seeds, fruit, and sometimes small insects
LIFESPAN	Up to 14 years

The exotic Sudan golden sparrow has an air of perky defiance that is celebrated by bird lovers. The male's bright yellow feathers help him to attract a mate.

WHERE IN THE WORLD?

Lives in dry savanna and scrublands along the southern edge of the Sahara in Africa.

ANIMAL FACTS

The Sudan golden sparrow is a highly social bird. It gathers in mixed flocks with other kinds of birds. Hundreds of thousands of these birds may gather in a single location, where they may damage crops. The birds usually feed on seeds, but they gather insects for their chicks. During the breeding season, the male's color brightens, and his bill becomes shiny black. The Sudan golden sparrow is also a popular pet. It is often called the golden song sparrow.

The male (top) has brighter feathers and a darker beak than the female (bottom).

BODY
Despite their exotic color, they are much like other sparrows in body shape, with a broad trunk, large head, and prominent bill.

FEATHERS
Males keep their bright feathers the year around, not just in the breeding season.

BILL
The bill is strong enough to crack open seed cases but nimble enough to catch the occasional insect.

HOW BIG IS IT?

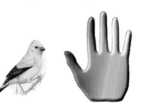

MASTER ARCHITECT

The nest is built by the male over several days. The quality of his building skills helps him attract a mate. The birds have learned to use stiff twigs to provide ventilation and drainage during the flash floods that can strike dry areas of the savanna.

Jackson's Widowbird

VITAL STATISTICS

WEIGHT	Males: 1.4–1.7 oz (40–49 g). Females: 1–1.5 oz (29–42 g)
LENGTH	5.5 in (14 cm)
SEXUAL MATURITY	3 years
INCUBATION PERIOD	13 days
FLEDGLING PERIOD	15 days
NUMBER OF EGGS	2–3 eggs
NUMBER OF BROODS	1 a year
HABITS	Active at day
TYPICAL DIET	Seeds and some insects

ANIMAL FACTS

This bird's name comes from the appearance of the breeding male. It resembles the black silk dresses worn by widows in the Victorian era (1837-1901). During the breeding season, many males clear an area of grass. Throwing its head back and arching its tail feathers, the male jumps repeatedly. Females pick a mate based on the length of his tail and the quality of his jumping dance. The nest is a woven ball of grass built near the ground. These birds are *threatened* (in danger of being wiped out) by the spread of agriculture.

The breeding female is drab in comparison with the male.

For most of the year, male Jackson's widowbirds are ordinary brown birds. With the arrival of the breeding season, they grow long plumes and perform elaborate courtship dances.

WHERE IN THE WORLD?

Found only in central Kenya and northern Tanzania.

BILL
The short, wedge-shaped bill is an excellent tool for crushing seeds from grasses.

BODY
These light, delicate perching birds can support themselves on plant stems.

TAIL
The beautiful tail feathers of the breeding male can grow up to 5.9 inches (15 centimeters) long.

HOW BIG IS IT

DRESSED FOR SUCCESS

The male Jackson's widowbird spares no effort in attracting a mate. He loses his everyday feathers and dresses all in black, with long tail plumes. He performs elaborate courtship dances, jumping while holding his black tail plumes over his back.

Southern Red Bishop

VITAL STATISTICS

LENGTH	4.7–5.5 in (12–14 cm)
SEXUAL MATURITY	1 year
INCUBATION PERIOD	11–14 days
FLEDGLING PERIOD	13–16 days
NUMBER OF EGGS	3 eggs per nest
CALL	Wheezing squeaks
HABITS	Active at day
TYPICAL DIET	Seeds and insects
LIFESPAN	Up to 15 years

The vivid red *plumage* (feathers) of the male southern red bishop looks like a wild poppy growing among the grass of the African savanna. But the bird takes its name from the robes sometimes worn by bishops.

WHERE IN THE WORLD?

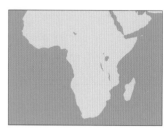

Common in the savannas of southern Africa, as far north as southern Uganda. Absent from southwestern deserts.

ANIMAL FACTS

Male and female red bishops look so different that it may be hard to believe they belong to the same *species* (kind). They spend most of the year in dry savanna. During the breeding season, the males grow their vividly colored feathers. The birds often move to wetlands, where the males build several nests made of reeds and other plant matter. Males puff up their feathers, dance, and make a whirring sound to attract mates. Males typically breed with several females. The bird is social and often forms large flocks with other species.

The female is brown and pale, without the vivid colors of the breeding male.

HEAD
Longer feathers on the head and neck form a fluffy ruff around the bird's throat.

WINGS
During courtship displays, male red bishops hover in the air, making a whirring sound that comes from vibrations of the feathers on their wing tips.

BILL
The red bishop's short, wedge-shaped bill is well suited to crushing seeds from grasses.

HOW BIG IS IT?

TRAVELING LIGHT

Southern red bishops have short, rounded tails, which help them to move rapidly through heavy grass. These shorter tails make them less maneuverable in flight. However, longer feathers would get in their way in the grass.

Yellow-Billed Oxpecker

Oxpeckers are also known as tickbirds because they feed on troublesome ticks and insects that infest large mammals. But the birds also irritate wounds on the animals' skin and drink their blood.

VITAL STATISTICS

WEIGHT	2 oz (60 g)
LENGTH	8 in (20 cm)
SEXUAL MATURITY	1 year
INCUBATION PERIOD	Around 12 days
NUMBER OF EGGS	2–3 eggs
NUMBER OF BROODS	1 a year
CALL	Hissing "krisss" cry
HABITS	Active at day
TYPICAL DIET	Ticks, insects, and the blood of its hosts

WHERE IN THE WORLD?

Lives in Africa south of the Sahara. It is most common in central Africa, but it also occurs in some areas in the south.

ANIMAL FACTS

Yellow-billed oxpeckers have a taste for blood. They feed mainly on ticks that infest the skin of such large mammals as oxen and wildebeests. These ticks are usually engorged with blood taken from the grazing animal. Removing the ticks benefits the animal host. But oxpeckers also sip blood from the open wounds. In fact, their pecking keeps the wounds open, which contributes to fresh infestations of ticks. Oxpeckers are so dependent on grazing animals that they even spend the night on them, *roosting* (sleeping) on their backs.

Differences in bill color and the ring around the eye distinguish the yellow-billed oxpecker (left) from its close relative, the red-billed oxpecker (right).

BILL
Their scissor-shaped bills are well suited to digging ticks and insects out of the hides of grazing animals.

EYE
The eyes are a vivid shade of red, similar in color to the tip of the bill.

BODY
The body is light, as is typical of perching birds. Feathers on the back are dark, with light brown underparts.

HOW BIG IS IT?

GETTING A GRIP

Oxpeckers are well suited to life on the move. Long, stiff tail feathers help them to keep their balance as they perch on their host's back to feed. Short legs and feet, tipped with sharp claws, also ensure that they have a good, strong grip.

Red-Billed Oxpecker

Buphagus erythrorhynchus

VITAL STATISTICS

LENGTH	8–8.6 in (20–22 cm)
SEXUAL MATURITY	1 year
INCUBATION PERIOD	12–14 days
FLEDGLING PERIOD	26–30 days
NUMBER OF EGGS	1–5 eggs
NUMBER OF BROODS	1 a year
CALLS	Hissings and short twittering calls
TYPICAL DIET	Ticks, insects, and the blood of its hosts

Like yellow-billed oxpeckers, these birds feast on ticks and insects that live on the bodies of large African mammals. Several birds may search for food on the back of a single grazing animal.

WHERE IN THE WORLD?

Found mostly in southern and eastern Africa, following the movements of herds of grazing animals.

ANIMAL FACTS

Oxpeckers depend on large *mammals* (animals that feed their young on the mother's milk) for food and even a place to *roost* (sleep) at night. Scientists describe such a close relationship as *symbiosis,* which means *living together.* Such relationships may benefit both parties. But they sometimes benefit only one animal. For instance, the ticks that feed on grazing animals also have a symbiotic relationship with their hosts, but they cause only harm. By eating ticks, oxpeckers may benefit their hosts, but they also keep skin wounds open and feed on the animals' blood.

The juvenile has an olive-colored bill.

BODY
With a long, slender neck and a streamlined body, the bird is about the same size as a starling.

FEET
Short legs and long feet tipped with sharp claws enable the bird to keep its grip on the body of a moving animal.

TAIL
Long, stiff tail feathers help the bird to keep its balance as it perches on its host's body. The bird can even maintain its balance on the neck of a giraffe.

HOW BIG IS IT?

AN EYE FOR DANGER

In addition to removing ticks, oxpeckers provide another service to grazing animals. The birds give a loud alarm call when they see a *predator* (hunting animal) sneaking up on the herd. Thus, the oxpeckers provide an early warning system. This may help to explain why grazing animals tolerate oxpeckers, despite the birds' taste for blood.

Melodious Warbler

VITAL STATISTICS

WEIGHT	0.4 oz (13 g)
LENGTH	4.7–5 in (12–13 cm)
WINGSPAN	7 in (18 cm)
SEXUAL MATURITY	1 year
INCUBATION PERIOD	12–13 days
FLEDGLING PERIOD	11–13 days
NUMBER OF EGGS	3–4 eggs
NUMBER OF BROODS	1–2 a year
HABITS	Active at day
TYPICAL DIET	Insects plus some fruit in autumn

ANIMAL FACTS

Melodious warblers spend much of the year in western Europe. They favor open forests around rivers and streams. Their short wings enable them to maneuver among the trees as they search for insect prey. They take insects from leaves and snatch them in mid-air. Before winter comes, all the warblers *migrate* (travel) to the savannas of western Africa. There, the birds build nests in small trees or bushes. The nest is a deep cup made of plant stems and leaves. It may be lined with feathers, hair, and even spider webs. The chicks are able to fly less than two weeks after hatching.

Melodious warblers create pleasant songs. They often weave the songs of other birds into their own melodies.

WHERE IN THE WORLD?

Migrates to western Africa, south of the Sahara, for the winter. Summers in western Europe and northwestern Africa.

CAMOUFLAGE
The adult's yellow-green breeding coloration enables it to blend in with the leaves of trees.

WINGS
These are short and rounded, enabling it to fly among trees. The tail aids balance and ability to maneuver.

FEET
Like other perching birds, the feet of this warbler are well suited to grasping twigs and plant stems.

HOW BIG IS IT?

WINGING IT

Many birds that migrate for the winter have long wings that are suited to long-distance travel. However, melodious warblers make only relatively short migrations. As a result, their wings can be short, a feature that helps them to maneuver in wooded areas.

Whinchat

VITAL STATISTICS

WEIGHT	0.6 oz (17 g)
LENGTH	4.7 in (12 cm)
WINGSPAN	8.7 in (22 cm)
SEXUAL MATURITY	1 year
INCUBATION PERIOD	13 days
FLEDGLING PERIOD	14–15 days
NUMBER OF EGGS	5–6 eggs
NUMBER OF BROODS	1 a year, but a second may be laid if the first clutch fails
TYPICAL DIET	Eats mainly insects, along with some fruit
LIFESPAN	1 year

Whinchats perch on twigs or other vegetation, but they are lively birds. They often run and hop across the ground as they search for insect prey.

WHERE IN THE WORLD?

Migrates (travels) to central and eastern Africa for the winter. Spends the rest of the year in Europe and western Asia.

ANIMAL FACTS

Whinchats feed mainly on insects and insect *larvae* (young). The larvae are usually caught on the ground, but adult insects are often captured in flight. The birds also sometimes feed on small snails, spiders, and worms. Winchats also may be caught in flight by birds of prey. Other *predators* (hunting animals) include stoats and weasels. Cuckoos may lay their own eggs in the whinchat's nest. The cuckoo chicks hatch early and push the whinchat's eggs out of the nest. They are remarkable mimics, imitating the cries of whinchat chicks to trick the parents into feeding the intruders.

Whinchats are able to snatch insect prey in mid-flight.

WINGS
Male whinchats have white patches on their wings. The females usually lack such patches.

COLORATION
Male whinchats have streaked brown upperparts. The underparts are often described as apricot in color. A white band highlights the eyes.

TAIL
Whinchats have a relatively short tail, which they often flick nervously as they perch on twigs or other vegetation.

HOW BIG IS IT?

DON'T TREAD ON ME

Whinchats nest on the ground, among tall grasses. These nests are *camouflaged* (disguised), for crows and magpies will steal and eat eggs from any nest they find. Nests also may be trampled by livestock.

Ostrich

VITAL STATISTICS

WEIGHT	220–353 lb (100–160 kg)
HEIGHT	Males: 5.9–8.8 ft (1.8–2.7 m) Females: 5.6–6.6 ft (1.7–2 m)
WINGSPAN	6.6 ft (2 m)
SEXUAL MATURITY	2–4 years
LAYS EGGS	April–September
INCUBATION PERIOD	35–45 days
FLEDGLING PERIOD	14–15 days
NUMBER OF EGGS	12–15 eggs per nest
TYPICAL DIET	Plants, roots, seeds; some insects and small reptiles
LIFESPAN	Usually less than 40 years

ANIMAL FACTS

The ostrich's long neck helps it to spot *predators* (hunting animals). Although it cannot fly, the ostrich runs so quickly that few predators can catch it. The male ostrich has an unusual voice. It can make a deep booming call. Both males and females may make deep hissing sounds when threatened. Male and female ostriches have many mates. Each male digs a shallow nest, and three to six females lay their eggs in the nest. Each hen lays as many as 10 eggs. The male sits on the eggs at night. During the day, a hen helps keep them warm. Ostrich plumes were once popular as decorations on hats and clothing. Today, ostriches are farmed for their eggs and meat, which tastes more like beef than the meat of other birds.

The ostrich is the world's largest living bird. It also lays the largest eggs, each of which is about 6 inches (15 centimeters) across and weighs 3 pounds (1.4 kilograms).

WHERE IN THE WORLD?

Found in central and southern Africa. Also farmed in Australia, Israel, South Africa, and the United States.

HEADS UP!

The belief that the ostrich hides its head in the sand when frightened is not true. This belief probably stems from the bird's habit of rearranging the eggs in its nest with its bill. From a distance, it may appear that the ostrich's head has disappeared into the sand.

WINGS
Despite having large wings, the ostrich cannot fly. Instead, it uses the wings in mating displays and to shade its chicks.

NECK
The scientific name for this bird comes from the Greek words for *camel sparrow,* a reference to its long neck.

LEGS
The strong legs can cover 10 to 16 feet (3 to 5 meters) in a single stride. The bird can also deliver powerful kicks to defend itself from predators.

HOW BIG IS IT?

SPECIAL ADAPTATION

The ostrich is the only bird that has only two toes on each foot. Its springlike feet help the bird to run quickly on the savanna. The ostrich can reach speeds of about 40 miles (64 kilometers) per hour.

Black Mamba

VITAL STATISTICS

WEIGHT	Up to 3.5 lb (1.6 kg)
LENGTH	Typically 8–10 ft (2.4–3 m), but has been known to reach 14.7 ft (4.5 m)
SEXUAL MATURITY	2 years
NUMBER OF EGGS	10–25, laid nearly 2 months after mating
INCUBATION PERIOD	2–3 months
DIET	Mainly small mammals such as squirrels and hyraxes
LIFESPAN	Up to 12 years

The black mamba is perhaps the fastest of all snakes, reaching speeds of more than 7 miles (11 kilometers) per hour. The powerful *venom* (poison) of a black mamba can kill a person in 20 minutes.

WHERE IN THE WORLD?

Widely distributed across eastern and southern parts of Africa, extending from Somalia to South Africa.

ANIMAL FACTS

The black mamba is among the most feared snakes of Africa. Their potent venom kills prey through paralysis, which makes it impossible to breathe. Fortunately, the snake avoids people and usually retreats. People who are bitten can be saved by *antivenin,* a substance made from venom that neutralizes its effects. During the breeding season, males fight for access to females. The males wrestle by rising up and *entwining* (interweaving) their bodies. The female lays her eggs in a *burrow* (underground shelter) and then abandons them. The young hatch ready to fend for themselves. They are deadly within minutes.

PROFILE
The body is long and the tail tapers toward the end.

SCALES
The largest scales are on the head.

EYES
Like other snakes, it lacks eyelids. Instead, the eyes are protected by a clear scale.

COLORATION
Despite their name, these snakes are usually gray. The name refers to the black interior of the mouth.

HUNTING STRATEGY
After biting its prey, the snake may release its victim and wait for the venom to take effect. Birds are generally not released, in case they fly away.

An organ in the roof of the mouth provides the snake with a keen sense of smell.

HOW BIG IS IT?

READY TO STRIKE
When threatened, the black mamba rises up and spreads a small hood. But the snakes are shy and usually retreat from people.

Bombardier Beetle

GENUS • *Brachinus*

These beetles are able to fire a cocktail of noxious, boiling hot chemicals at *predators* (hunting animals). This spray is painful to human skin and can be deadly to other insects.

VITAL STATISTICS

LENGTH	0.2–0.4 in (6.5–9.5 cm), depending on *species* (type)
SEXUAL MATURITY	Probably 3–6 weeks
NUMBER OF EGGS	1, laid in rotting wood or in soil
DEVELOPMENT PERIOD	Reaches adulthood in about 3 weeks
DIET	Feeds on insects and other small animals
LIFESPAN	3–6 weeks

ANIMAL FACTS

Bombardier beetles do not drop bombs on ants and other insects, but they are experts in chemical warfare. The beetles store two noxious chemicals in special *glands* (organs) in the abdomen. When threatened, the beetle releases these chemicals into a special chamber. The chemicals react violently, becoming a hot, toxic mist. The chemicals explode out of the chamber. Nozzles enable the beetle to aim the blast at a predator. The spray is boiling hot and can eat away at another insect's body. It also has an unpleasant odor. Few animals are willing to brave the beetle's toxic spray.

WHERE IN THE WORLD?

Can be found globally, both in mild and tropical climates, but is especially common in savannas, grasslands, and woodlands.

WINGS
Although primarily ground-dwelling, many bombardier beetles can fly. Becoming airborne is a relatively slow process, as the outer wing covers must be lifted first.

COLORATION
The brown and black coloration of these insects helps them to blend in with soil.

EYES
These beetles have large, black compound eyes.

ANTENNAE
Long antennae are mainly organs of smell but also feel out the environment.

HOW BIG IS IT?

CHEMICAL WARFARE
The beetle's toxic spray is often used against ants, but it may offer protection against lizards and larger animals.

46

Glossary

adaptation a characteristic of a living thing that makes it better able to survive and reproduce in its environment

antivenin a substance that counteracts a *venin* (a poisonous protein in the venom of snakes and other poisonous animals)

burrow a hole in the ground that an animal uses as a dwelling or hiding place

camouflage protective coloration that makes an animal difficult for a predator to see

carrion dead and decaying animal flesh

drag the force that acts on a body as it moves through air or water making it more difficult to move forward

extinction the condition of being no longer in existence; wiped out

foraging to hunt or search for food

game wild animals, birds, or fish hunted or caught for sport or for food

gland an organ that makes a particular substance that the body needs

grassland a region with mostly grass and few trees that is one of the four chief kinds of natural vegetation (along with forests, desert shrubs, and tundras); most grasslands lie between very arid lands, or deserts, and humid lands covered with forests, though some grasslands occur in humid climates

graze to feed on grass and other low-growing plants that cover a large extent of ground

habitat the kind of place in which an animal lives

hare an animal that resembles a rabbit but which is larger and does not burrow

harem a group of female animals controlled by one male

helmet large bony lump atop the head of some birds

incubate to keep fertilized eggs and young animals under proper conditions for growth and development

larva the immature form of certain animals, which differs from the adult form in many ways; crustaceans, fish, insects, and mollusks typically have a larval stage

mammal an animal that feeds its young on the mother's milk

migration the movement of animals from place to place to avoid unfavorable changes in weather or food supply, or to take advantage of better living conditions.

plumage the feathers of a bird

poacher a person who fishes or hunts animals illegally

predator an animal that preys upon other animals

pride a group of lions living together

raptor bird of prey

rodent a type of mammal with front teeth especially suited to gnawing hard objects

roosting a behavior in which such animals as bats or birds rest or sleep on a perch

savanna a grassland with widely scattered trees and shrubs found chiefly in the tropics and between deserts and rain forests; also spelled *savannah*

scavenger an animal that feeds on the remains of other animals; some scavengers also hunt fresh meat

species a kind of living thing; members of a species share many characteristics and are able to interbreed

symbiosis a relationship between two creatures in which at least one of them benefits

talon the claw of an animal, especially a bird of prey

terrain an area of land having certain natural features

territory an area within definite boundaries, such as a nesting ground, in which an animal lives and from which it keeps out others of its kind

venom a poisonous substance produced by many kinds of animals to injure, kill, or digest prey

wallow to roll about in water or mud, as pigs do

wattles fleshy patches on the cheeks of some birds

Resources

Books

African Critters by Robert B. Haas (National Geographic, 2008)
Beautiful photographs introduce readers to the animals of Africa's plains and savannas.

Savanna Food Chains by Bobbie Kalman and Hadley Dyer (Crabtree, 2007)
Explore how all the parts of the savanna are linked, and learn about the challenges Earth's savannas now face.

A Savanna Habitat by Bobbie Kalman and Rebecca Sjonger (Crabtree, 2007)
Take a closer look at the savanna and the animals that live there.

Websites

African Savanna
http://www.pittsburghzoo.org/AnimalsandExhibits
Learn about the animals of the savanna and how people are fighting to conserve their habitats at this site created by the Pittsburgh Zoo.

Biomes: Tropical Savannahs
http://www.cotf.edu/ete/modules/msese/earthsysflr/savannah.html
These pages explore the climate, terrain, and life of the savanna.

Spectacular Savannas
http://kids.sandiegozoo.org/spectacular_savannas
Check out videos and photos of savanna animals at this website from the San Diego Zoo.

Acknowledgments

Cover photograph: Alamy (Steve Bloom Images)

Illustrations: © Art-Tech

Photographs:

Richard Bartz: 29

Buiten-Beeld: 39 (Rob Nagtegaal), 41(Ran Schols)

Corbis RF: 18, 20, 22, 23

Dreamstime: 10 (Stephen Foerster), 16 (J. G. Swanepoel), 35 (I. Konoval)

FLPA: 13 (R. Du Toit), 26 (J. and C. Sohns), 27 (ZZSD), 28 (Frans Lanting), 36 (F. Merlet), 37 (David Hosking), 45 (N. Cattlin)

Fotolia: 32 (K. Wendorf), 40 (D. Garry)

Getty RF: 31, 34

iStock Photo: 30 (G. Shimmin), 33 (E. Snow), 38 (P. Pazzi), 44 (M. Kostich)

Artur Mikolajenski: 42

Photos.com: 6, 7, 9, 11, 12, 14, 15, 17, 19, 21, 24, 25, 43

Stock.Xchng: 8 (Ned Benjamin)

Index